Which Values?

SECOND – POST-OPTIMISM – EDITION

Woody Wood

Devolve!

Leicester, England

Published by *Devolve!*
13 Biddulph Street
Leicester
England
LE2 1BH

Which Values? / Woody Wood — 2nd edition

ISBN 978-0-9931126-4-5

Cover design and Typography by Falcon Oast Graphic Art Ltd.

Printed and bound by imprintdigital.com

Other publications by *Devolve!* in this series: -

Values for Our Time   ISBN 978-0-9931126-0-7

Which Values? (first edition)   ISBN 978-0-9931126-1-4

A Journey into A Future   ISBN 978-0-9931126-2-1

The Limitations of
Enlightenment Science   ISBN 978-0-9931126-3-8

All distributed by Central Books Ltd.

www.centralbooks.com   44 (0)20 8525 8800

To the late Jack Parsons

for his exploration of values in

'Population versus Liberty'

for his examination of the work

of Thomas Robert Malthus

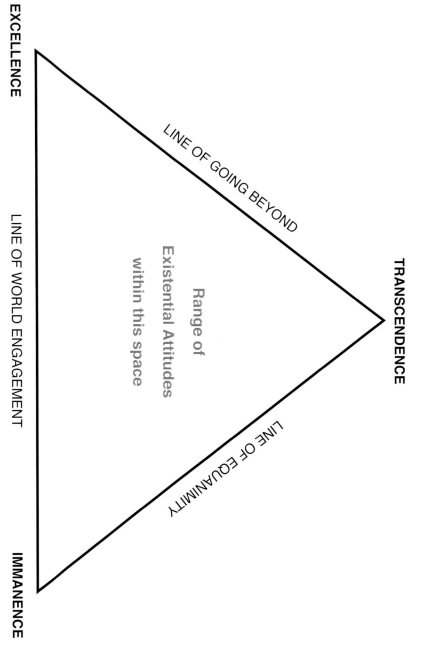

SPACE GEOGRAPHY: THE ETI TRIANGLE
Existential Attitudes To Life

EXCELLENCE

TRANSCENDENCE

IMMANENCE

LINE OF GOING BEYOND

LINE OF EQUANIMITY

LINE OF WORLD ENGAGEMENT

Range of
Existential Attitudes
within this space

WHICH VALUES?

SECOND – POST-OPTIMISM - EDITION

FRONT NOTE

The essay *Values for Our Time*[1], first drafted in 2010–11 and modified by critical feedback up to late 2014, attempted to be dispassionate.

Having disposed at the start with the myth of disinterested objective knowledge (as have critical scientists and others[2]) it also strove to avoid subjective viewpoints and prejudices in favour of motivated understanding: biased only by the problems that it was attempting to solve.

A consequence of this was that despite being driven by a growing concern (shared by many) for the future of life on our planet the essay did not recommend any one way forward. After exploring natural and social structures it merely noted the values shift likely to be needed and defined as 'values warriors' those ready to argue for those values. It listed at the end some possible courses of human action, their probabilities and their estimated effects on the future. Thus *Values for Our Time* (henceforth abbreviated to *VFOT)* has been criticised for "not coming off the fence".

So the present essay is to be read as a supplement to that exploration (ideally with *VFOT* to hand) in which i lay out my commitment to a response based on my understanding as of now; a further exploration of the values needed to support that response.

*   *   *   *   *   *   *   *   *

As of 2019 the availability of a wider range of wisdoms and insights plus indications that the balance of probability now suggests a radical transition point for Planet Earth ... has prompted this less optimistic and somewhat expanded edition of *Which Values?*

Reprise on the Natural World Story of *Values for Our Time*

THE UNIVERSE AND VALUES

In the Natural World Story of *VFOT* the sixth pattern of our Universe to be identified indicated that the Universe has an inside as well as an outside. This was supported by linking our own self-experience of our feelings, wishes and fears to Schopenhauer's[3] insight in his *The World as Will and Idea*. This was published in 1819. In today's language this might be translated as 'The Universe as both Passion and Object'.

In that same story the concept 'subjective' was rejected as downplaying our self-experience of the inside of the Universe as trivial in comparison with the attempt of science to measure and theorise on the outside of the Universe, the object. (Several critics have pointed out[4] that 'science', especially in its pre-quantum classical mode, is strictly an ideology, while its unspoken wider assumptions rank it as a cosmology. There is an ironic twist in that the science of 'true facts' is still foundational in the social sciences whereas many physicists have moved on.)

So our first emphasis is on the *parity* of the inside of the Universe (where we ourselves glimpse feeling, willing and suffering) and the outside of the Universe (where we can observe, note patterns, do calculations).

Going Forward

However, some impressions given in the Natural World Story now need correcting and taking further. In *VFOT* it was claimed that we experience the inside of the Universe through our feelings. It would be fairer to say that our experiences are of mere fringes, shorelines of that great ocean that is the self-experiencing Universe.

Elsewhere in that Story the point was made that morality arises when there is *any* conflict of goals; most especially for us as social group animals when our goals and ambitions come into conflict with the goals and norms of our social group, which we may have partly internalised.

To a Freudian[5] this latter conflict is between our drives "I want" and our super-egos "I ought not". Of course we judge others morally on their behaviour as do other social group animals. The cry of the four year old "that's not fair!" is much older than language.

Beyond Absolutes

Now in *VFOT* i take responsibility for rejecting all absolutes, all categorical imperatives, parachuted in from nowhere. In a relative Universe all morality is relative to a purpose, whether a god's purpose or a people's 'table of values' [cf Nietzsche] or the purposes of a priest class or ruling elite.

So the conviction of many writers, social philosophers and indeed people generally that there is a deep sense in which some behaviour is 'absolutely' morally wrong, is 'evil', is to be declared as error … or is it?

If the notion of the inside of the Universe as its experiencing side, encompassing and integrating all the experiences and feelings of its parts, *is* valid, then this could include an integrative purpose with its attendant morality.

Putting this in other language: if human (and other) minds can be thought of as computers; their operations as goal seeking willing activity; their feedback loops as suffering sensing … where is the server?

It is at least a plausible hypothesis that in this sense the Universe experiences itself, enjoys itself, suffers itself – and therefore any experiences that offend its optimising purpose likewise offend its universal morality.

This tentative model should not be pushed too far, yet it would account for certain natural and social features.

For example, the conviction that biological evolution is *completely* explained by natural (i.e. statistical) selection of random variations and mutations is now only held by un-reconstructed Neo-Darwinists. There is general recognition that something else is going on but no widely accepted explanation. Ability, at the level of biology, for nature to draw down wisdom already 'out there' (or rather 'in here') would fit with the truly creative evolution process that we observe.

For another example, the widespread understanding of sages and mystics of the importance of being 'in touch with the centre' would certainly fit the hypothesis. The response of the sceptical Western mind to this wisdom, these wisdoms, is to 'park it all in a box over there and leave well alone'.

It is a matter of regret that i was not aware of Lawrence LeShan's[6] challenging exploration in *'The Medium, The Mystic and the Physicist'* when attempting a coherent story in *VFOT*.

That work combines rigorous practical proofs of 'paranormal' events, notably in healing, with a broader explanation that – to his personal discomfort – goes way beyond what is acceptable to conventional science in its implications.

Now the hypothesis of an inner, experiencing side to our Universe is one way of understanding our situation. (This, along with other views, is explored later under cosmology.)

* * * * * * * * *

Some Roads

At the close of the Third Story of *VFOT* six possible response strategies were outlined. (There may of course be others.) These are now revisited with some personal comments.

Let me now state clearly that i reject eugenics and bioengineering as responses. These might certainly bring human numbers down fast but would be further examples of humans playing god with nature instead of being humble partners – just what got the biosphere into its current trajectory.

A further option listed in *VFOT* was 'escape to another planet'. Apart from its practical impossibility at the present level of technology and the likely demise of the high complexity social and technical structures required for such a mission, the thought of unleashing the virus called Homo sapiens on the rest of the galaxy is a sobering one.

The 'do nothing' option was given as very probable. Strictly meaning 'do nothing effective' as governments in particular would attempt to balance demands of their populations (whether electorates or not) against pressure from lobbies.

From an ecocentric standpoint the lack of any work to challenge values, even among minorities, would mean that the same proportions of homocentric and 'me-centric' attitudes would be carried forward among survivors of the step change.

The most shocking conclusion was that 'strong environmental action' as advocated by most ecologically conscious thinkers and activists could actually have the effect of *delaying* the human population decline, maintaining the pressure of human activity on the rest of the biosphere for longer.

This provocative statement needs to be qualified in two ways.

Certain actions that do check the rate of destruction of the biosphere and the creature web in the near term, rather than just improve prospects for humans, might contribute to eventual recovery. For example halting the destruction of rain forests. For another example stopping plastic from entering the oceans.

The other qualifier concerns the important question of the proportions of arrogant, dominating attitudes to nature as against a sense of humble partnership based on honouring the enchantment all around us. The shorthand for weighing these two ways of being in the world is the *values mix* – especially among survivors of the population decline. It can certainly be argued that the awakening to Gaia's pain within sub-cultures of environmental activism will contribute to more humility in the later values mix.

Notwithstanding these caveats it remains true that the longer the demands of many billions of humans continue to extract resources from and pollute our biosphere the greater the overall impoverishment and the slower the recovery.

The last of the listed options to be considered was "values shift by (some) humans to an ecocentric stance". How realistic is this? And what does 'values shift' mean in this context?

Now closely linked to values and changing values is *identification*. What you (we) identify with determines your (our) loyalties and values.

Values Shift, Values Drift

Taking the last question first, it was argued in the Natural World Story of *VFOT* that morality arises when there is *any* conflict of goals and possible behaviours, even within an individual. However it is mainly thought of as a social phenomenon, reflecting the conflict of goals and behaviours between social groups *or* between sectional interests within social groups *or* conflicting memes (mental programmes) embedded in sub-sets within those groups.

In traditional human societies there were *three* value patterns relevant to their situation (all important). First, loyalty to the hunting group or tribe, with a closing of ranks in the face of adversity or threat. Second – internally – a sense of fair play; the precursor of justice. Third, those groups were closely embedded in nature, in their natural surroundings. They were intensely aware of the wonder, the enchantment, yet also of the terrible power that could be unleashed. Hence the value of awe and respect that was to give rise to the first nature gods.

Through the course of human social evolution key changes or stages may be noted. The gods, once a synonym for nature, were projected onto the sky and then beyond the sky, becoming remote from earthly nature.

The birth of agriculture led to massive populations, unthinkable for hunter-gatherers, with class/cultural exploitation in stratified societies. Priest castes co-opted religion to their own ends. Mighty nations hijacked the deeply embedded value of group identity to their advantage. The notion of fair play between kindred was trumped by the inclusion of alien others, often as slaves, within the state hegemony. No wonder Norman O. Brown[7] could write: "human history is not a process of becoming wiser but a process of becoming sicker"

The second stage of this evolution saw the rise to prominence of new values.

With nature relegated to the side lines, to a 'resource', an increasingly arrogant humanity now worshipped 'progress': incorporating science, money and power, as its new gods. The breakdown of fraternal bonds in increasingly cosmopolitan societies led to the growth of two conflicting values; opposing moralities. On the one hand rampant individualism and self-interest – at first attempting to wear other clothes, more recently flaunting its ascendancy and self-assurance. On the other hand the extension of the original instincts of empathy with kin into identification with losers everywhere, with the oppressed of the Earth. (Slave morality in Nietzsche's language[8].) Hence the original value of intra-tribal fair play morphed into liberal values with universal aspirations.

Significantly these two apparently opposite poles – self-interest and underdog identification – are able to recombine under the banner of individual freedom from oppression and tyranny. Hence the two very different interpretations of 'libertarian'.

The Values Challenge

For those of us seeking to support a relative increase in Planet Centred Values at this critical time the above story gives both encouragement and challenge.

The narrative confirms other work arguing that the dominant values in human social groups are subject to change and that these shifts are in part a response to structural and situational changes within and without – an interpretation with which most Marxists would concur.

What circumstances are arising now that could complement influence by argument and example? Or, using other language, that could extend the subjective group[9] to Planet Centred values? We can note some of these as encouraging signs: -

➢ Growing awareness of the plight of Planet Earth now reaches beyond concerned minorities into populist culture (thanks to 'newsworthy' events) even if implications are not brought out.

➢ Within several religious movements there is a conscious attempt to reconnect with nature (often by re-interpretation of traditional texts). [Paganism has always celebrated the Earth and its mysteries.]

➢ Meanwhile, among some ordinary people there is a reaching out for meaning and connection.

➢ The social model that promised a better life for all is now suspect. Beyond this, the whole project of modernity, implying endless progress through the deconstruction of mystery and the conquest of nature, is coming under scrutiny despite spectacular advances in some areas and the increasingly shrill cries of its defenders.

➢ Plus of course, when things (from a human standpoint) really start falling apart one of the first casualties for many will be faith in existing mainstream values.

Alas, neo-liberal morality is now deeply embedded in our own psyches. Challenging it in *ourselves* from the standpoint of the needs of our biosphere, of Planet Earth, will be difficult enough without coping with the hostility of its committed defenders. We need also to keep in mind that we might just be wrong!

The Fabian Fallacy

The counterpoint to the rise of individual morality and the weakening of social communities and social bonds – formerly underpinned by strong social moralities – was the rise of the intrusive state …

The modern state now claims a monopoly of social power, increasingly usurping regional, local, community and family jurisdictions. No wonder the radical Jacobins and their Marxist heirs saw the capture of the state as the first pre-requisite of social improvement. Even where violence was explicitly rejected, social reformers such as the Fabians (in England) felt that state legislation was essential to 'impose' a fairer society upon us.

The weaker version of this Fabian Fallacy, still dominant in our age, is that bringing lobby pressure on political structures is the only way forward. The idea that we have it in us to self-organise, create structures that enable us to live out our values, seems fantasy to most of us today. Yet that is what the Victorian working classes were doing in the mid-1800s until the Fabian 'progressive' middle classes dismantled their achievements[10].

It's all about values, moralities. Fact: poverty could be abolished overnight if we all chose to share – or even partially share – our incomes. [Some of us actually do!] And all this without the permission of the state, without breaking the state's laws.

Seen in this context the values shift to a morality of humble partnership with nature is not so fanciful, once we realise that the resistance is in our heads. Don't blame the wicked corporations. Or rather, do blame them: we created them with our individualist 'laissez faire' moralities.

The Structure of Social Groups

Perhaps the first piece of homework for would-be values warriors is to review our understanding of social *structure*, of the criss-crossing network of social types (based on various criteria) and of the interactions and relations *between* these types. [Some of the following is covered in greater depth in the Social Story of *VFOT*.]

A weakness of almost all social theory hitherto is the serious weight placed on the human individual as the basic unit of society (even more so in the ego-driven age of individualism) and the relegation of social groupings to mere abstractions.

Now it was noted in that essay that any model of fixed social types breaks down under scrutiny, especially when small numbers are involved, into *modes* of social behaviour, dependant on situations. Notwithstanding this, it is still useful to speak of social types when taking a broader view of social process.

For the present purpose just three social type models will be noted: each valid in its own terms; each contributing some insights on social structure and social process (flow); each having distinctive key criteria by which its types are defined.

Social Structure 1 : Resistives and Sensitives

The first, a two stage model, was developed by Wilfred Trotter[11] (1872-1939) notably in his book *Instincts of The Herd in Peace and War.* It was concerned with the question of leadership, especially the failure of leadership in (mainly English) society.

Its first distinction was between an *undifferentiated* majority, 95%, 'the yeomen of England', who could just get on with their lives and their trades; deserving to be better led ... and a *differentiated* minority, 5%, who were the potential leaders of society.

The second argument was that within the 5% there were two distinct types/approaches to life. The first of these sub-types, whom Trotter labelled as *resistive*, were confident in themselves and their views; knew what was right; were capable of decisive leadership. The downside was that they were resistant to new ideas and new approaches to problems – hence 'resistive'.

The second sub-type was given the ironic title of *mentally unstable* by Trotter. They were more capable of what we might today call lateral thinking – considering alternative ways of looking at the world and new possible approaches to problems. The potential gain is obvious. The downside in this case was that being open minded and sceptical they found it difficult to commit to any one course of action as the right one and so to act decisively on it. Hence in the eyes of resistives, who knew what to do, they were clearly 'mentally unstable'.

Wilfred Trotter's core argument was that both these sub-types had something to bring to the table – and that if it were possible to integrate them within leadership structures then there was the prospect of bold and confident yet also flexible and visionary leadership.

A note on terminology and consequences. When this model was taken forward as a social experiment in a small group context[12] (which itself weakened the integrity of the model) 'resistive' became 'executive' and a mode of operating rather than a social type. Likewise 'mentally unstable' became 'sensitive' with 'sensory' as a meeting style of discussing issues and problems in depth without attempting executive decisions.

Social Structure 2 : Convergents and Divergents

The second model now considered was developed, or rather evolved, out of bitter experiences within the 1970s communities movement. Later it was taken up as an aid to social understanding by what was to become *Devolve!*[13] – a devolution movement morphing into a think tank with broadening interests.

The key parameters were power and responsibility – strictly *powerlessness* and *responsibility*. Terms for the two critical types – *Convergents* and *Divergents* – were borrowed from educational psychology where they have somewhat different meanings. (Two further types in the full theory need not be considered here.)

Of these two social types (sometimes better understood as social *modes* of behaviour in small group situations) the majority Convergents were assessed as making up about 95% of the social mix and the minority Divergents the other 5%. (These ratios turn up in a range of macro social models and experiments.)

The core behavioural difference was that Divergents were usually so challenged by the prospect of powerlessness that they were willing to take on responsibility in social situations: hence their alternative description as 'leaderful'. In contrast the majority Convergents were normally so anxious to avoid the stress of social responsibility that they were willing to abdicate their potential social power to others while usually enjoying proxy power by identification with leading Divergents: so the alternative label of 'followful'.

The *VFOT* essay identified other psychological advantages for the convergent stance. More relevant was the insight that this 'partnership' of leaderful and followful types could be socially stable; that under appropriate conditions it defines the basic structure of the human social group. The commonest threat to that social stability, first observed in the commune but applicable throughout society, was and is ego rivalries between leading Divergents dragging rival 'tribes' in their wake. Since often each faction will claim 'right on their side' and have a social/ political stance the polarity readily becomes a conflict of values.

Social Structure 3 : Spiral Dynamics Colour Memes

The third model reviewed briefly here (also treated in greater depth in *VFOT*) is the *Colour Meme* theory of Spiral Dynamics, developed in the US by Clare W Graves[14] and others. It should be said at the outset that Memes (strictly Super Memes or vMemes) are here social descriptions intended to apply to large groups of people – a long way from the quasi-biological usage of 'meme' as a replicator that is meant to be the software equivalent of the human gene.

VERY ROUGH TIMELINE (W. EUROPE)	DOMINANT WORLDVIEW of the EPOCH	DIVERGENT MINORITY PRINCIPAL ROUTE TO FULFILMENT/POWER	NEAREST S.D. MEME EQUIVALENT	CONVERGENT MAJORITY PRINCIPAL RESPONSE BEHAVIOURS	NEAREST S.D. MEME EQUIVALENT
10,000 BCE	IMMANENT NATURE	Leadership by Maturity, Moral Courage and Wisdom	NONE	Respect for Elders, Playfulness and Law of Least Effort Satisfaction In Work/Play Cycles Fear of Natural Dangers/Spirits	MODIFIED PURPLE
4,000 BCE	NATURE GODDESSES / GODS	Either: Power by The Sword: Ruthlessness, Courage In Battle Or: Power from Magic/ Religion: Dispensing Safety/Salvation	RED	Loyalty, Obedience, sometimes Fanaticism and Scapegoating But also: Satisfaction In Trade or Craft and in Celebrations	STAGE 1 BLUE
500 CE	TRANSCEND-ENTAL GODHEAD		RED		STAGE 1 BLUE
1500 CE	RATIONAL OPTIMISM	Power from Wealth: Trade, Property/ Ownership, Labour Surplus Value, Usury (but backed up by The Sword)	ORANGE	Mercenaries, Jobsworths, Moaners, above all Consumers But also: Satisfaction In Socially Valid Work and In Hobbies	STAGE 2 BLUE
1800 CE					
During 1900s	RATIONAL PESSIMISM/ CYNICISM	Power from Information: Network Hubs, Control of Flows, Control of Presented Images (but backed up by Ownership Power, and ultimately: The Sword).	MOCK YELLOW	Hyper Consumers: Including of Intangibles; Indulgent Therapies and Experiences New Mistrust of Others Sometimes joining New Cults and Protest Movements	MOCK GREEN
2050?		Minority: Challenging The System's Vision; Explorations beyond Eco Competition	YELLOW	But also: Trying to maintain The Content of Life via Social Routines	
THE TIPPING POINT: BREAKDOWN, CHAOS AND CONFUSION					
Future 'A'	FRAGMENTED	New Warlord Terror	RED	Fear, Obedience, Hysteria	BROKEN PURPLE
Future 'B'	HOLISTIC	New Wisdom and Courage: Leaderfulness in Small Groups in an Austerity Environment	MODIFIED CORAL	Work/Relaxation/ Celebration Cycles within Co-operative Small Groups In an Austere and sometimes Fearful Environment	MODIFIED TURQUOISE

I. *Types and Memes: Historical view of Convergent and Divergent behaviours matched to Spiral Dynamics colour Memes*

Like the two previous models, Spiral Dynamics Meme theory is a theory of interacting social types, so it also argues that all societies, like all organisms, have structure.

A distinctive feature is that the theory claims to be evolutionary and progressive with some colour groups superseding others as statistically more dominant in the course of historical time.

Another distinctive feature is that the sequence of colours alternates between collectivist and individualist (potentially leaderful) Memes, giving some resonance with the Convergent - Divergent model of *Devolve!* theory. [Plate I shows a chart matching Divergent leads and Convergent responses against Spiral Dynamics Colour Memes during historical time and into projected futures.] Based on social research in one country (the US) the central portions of the spiral (Mediaeval to present time) can claim to be credible and useful descriptions. However the extrapolation into 'primitive' societies and into an 'enlightened' future is open to question.

Sub Groups

In the Social Story of *VFOT* social psychology was criticised both for clinging to methods of 'scientific objectivity' not appropriate to its subject and for viewing society through the prism of human individuals; their needs and neuroses.

On the second count this general condemnation needs to be corrected.

At the same time my basic assertion that humans as a species sit astride the interface between full collectivity and individuality failed to offer any explanation of the ways in which social structures respond to this polarity.

I have since become aware of explorations in this field which do take complex social structure seriously, viewing the dynamic from both ends, so to speak.

An insightful example of placing psychological needs in the context of complex social structure can be found in D.W. Harding[15]. Very relevant to our concerns is the discussion of sub groups[16] within whole societies or cultures. The point is made that a social culture is an enabler for diverse and diverging human potentialities which may then find both practical support and values approval or endorsement in sub groups of fairly like-minded others.

Harding states that: "A social matrix of shared values, companionship and emotional support seems to be a necessary condition for most social development and it is this that sub groups provide." He goes further: "Group psychology, especially when a large community is in question, is sub group psychology."

Now the concept of Civil Society was contrasted in *VFOT* with both The State and The Market. It was noted

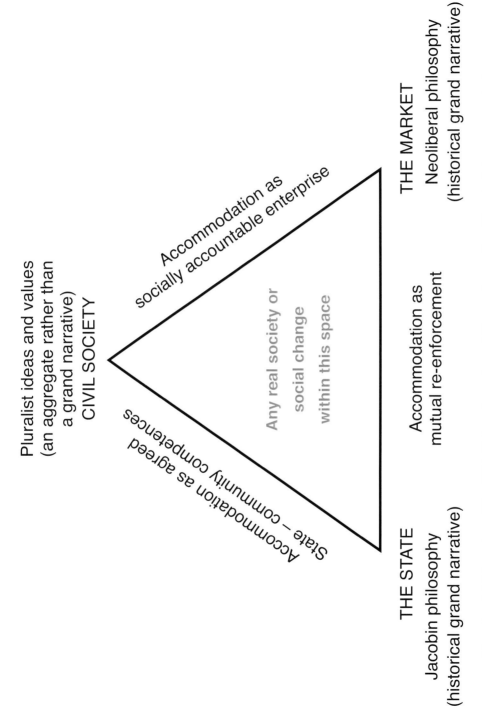

Pluralist ideas and values
(an aggregate rather than
a grand narrative)
CIVIL SOCIETY

Accommodation as
socially accountable enterprise

THE MARKET
Neoliberal philosophy
(historical grand narrative)

Any real society or
social change
within this space

Accommodation as
mutual re-enforcement

Accommodation as agreed
State – community competences

THE STATE
Jacobin philosophy
(historical grand narrative)

II. Social Mapping: The TSA Triangle – Grand Narratives: Conflict and Accommodation

that both the state model and the market model were underpinned by grand narratives or ideologies which their advocates sought to defend and impose. In contrast Civil Society cold never be more than an aggregate of pluralist ideas and values.

What the social psychology exampled by Harding achieves is to put content into the Civil Society notion.

The naive parallel with organic biological structures, where the parts serve the whole, is rejected in favour of a two way relation. Both the sub groups and the individual members are active in pursuing their ideals and interests even as they contribute diversity and richness to the culture as a whole. Thus a pluralist culture or wider society may be seen as an enabler that allows, creates space for, many and varied bonded sub groups – which in turn allow individuals to achieve undreamt of potentials in many directions.

Viewed in this light the failure of even the most idealistic communism (including the 'primitive communism' supposed by Karl Marx) to fulfil the needs and potentials of its human members becomes glaringly obvious. Also viewed in this light the 'free' market, which tends to reduce all human relations to a cash nexus between alienated individuals in a 'winner takes all' framework, permits only one dimensional fulfilment (for some) via material consumption and acquisition.

It was argued in *VFOT* that a partial mitigation is achieved in real, actual societies because The State and The Market rarely exist in pure forms: there is always some measure of compromise, both with each other and with residual Civil Society. Plate 12 of VFOT is reproduced in this essay as plate II.

For Harding a key consequence of the two way relation described above is that any culture may be judged inadequate to the needs of its members, to be failing its members (notably by not enabling their latent potentials) just as validly as individuals or sub groups may be judged as failing to contribute to the whole in a positive way. Interestingly no 'objective' criteria are identified to decide the issue. The point is merely made that the requirements of the wider group cannot be assumed to be the standard.

It should be added that the dynamics of interacting types (e.g. leaderful Divergents and followful Convergents) are even more potent – though also more problematic – in sub group contexts. Some of us learnt this the hard way in the alternative communities movement of the 1970s.

Social Mode Transformations

Another neglected dimension of social theory is that social groupings – from affinity groups to whole societies – can 'flip' from one mode of being, having characteristic values and attitudes, to another very different one. This is clearly of the utmost importance for those of us now arguing for Planet Centred values.

In the *VFOT* essay some key social modes were identified. These included 'fair play' or normal mode, 'war communism' or pull together mode, 'alienation' or individualist mode, 'feuding' or get you back mode, 'anarcho-panic' or social breakdown mode. A significant omission from the list was 'class tension' or polarised mode, which has frequently been dominant in England (say) over the centuries. [Social, economic and cultural class was examined under another heading.]

A classic example of a flip into war communism mode in England and the other home nations occurred in 1938 as the perceived threat from the Third Reich took hold. Even quasi-pacifists and rebel anarchists were now ready to fight Hitler.

More recently the Thatcher/Blair revolution heralded (or responded to?) a flip (or rather a slide) from socially cohesive 'fair play' to individualist 'alienation' mode. "Aspiration" is a coded tag for "devil take the hindmost".

Enchantment and Modernity

Anyone now viewing with dismay all the chickens coming home to roost (whether one's focus is only on the human predicament or on the larger catastrophe of the sixth extinction on our Planet) might reasonably ask "where did we go wrong?"

Any answer would partly depend on the timespan chosen. It could also be attempted in economic or social structure terms: in both cases with some validity. I would argue that underscoring both of these is a clash of values issue. More specifically of two ways of being in the World, of attitudes to the World. (This contrast is explored in a social context in the 'Community and Society' section below.)

One attitude, one set of values, can be grouped under the notion of *immanence*: being in the World, accepting the World, being enchanted by the World, suffering the World; knowing yourself (rather ourselves) as a little part of the big World.

The contrary attitude can be called instrumental: acting on the World, analysing the World, regulating the World, extracting from the World, mastering the World … the Universe no less; acting at all times towards the goal of more: more understanding, more control, more power, more wealth.

Now in our actual lives we need some of both. It could be hazardous to be entranced, transfixed, by the beauty of the sunset when night is coming and you haven't finished building your hut. It is a matter of apprehending the limits of both existential attitudes. In *VFOT* great prominence was given to the two thresholds principle of Ivan Illich and the importance, in so many spheres, of staying in the 'comfort zone' between the limiting dangers. [Plate VII gives a visual example.]

In large scale social terms, today global, the instrumental approach has come to be embodied in what can be called *modernity*: a triple alliance of techno-science, capitalism and the mega state. [At this point I wish to acknowledge a tremendous debt to Dr Patrick Curry for clarifying and sharpening my thinking in this area via his *Ecological Ethics*[17] and his collected essays in *Deep Roots in A Time of Frost*[18].]

Modernity has become an ideology: broader and more subtle than mere Neo-Liberalism. It has vociferous advocates, as scathing about the values of immanence – wilderness, localism, mystery, historic peoples and so on – as Karl Marx was about 'reactionaries'. Not just *an* ideology but the dominant ideology of today, the very air that most politicians, academics and market operators breathe. Today modernity is in part responsible for the destruction of our planet.

There is a tragic paradox at the heart of instrumentalism. By definition all its actions are intended to be instrumental towards goals: in sum a better future at the end of the rainbow. However, in the Natural World Story of *VFOT* the seventh pattern of our Universe was identified:

"every means strives to become an end"

Thus modernity in society, as the embodiment of instrumentalism, is not really transitory towards its supposed future. It is its own fulfilment.

This is not very cheerful stuff. Yet as values warriors we need to understand the size of the task in our struggle for appropriate values for our time. I agree with Patrick Curry[19] that one part of our response should lie in honouring enchantment in our World.

Community and Society

The contrast between two ways of being in the world has been recognised by several social observers. In *The Alienation of Modern Man* Fritz Pappenheim[20] draws attention to the ideas of Ferdinand Tönnies[21]

Tönnies' central concepts at the social level are Gemeinschaft and Gesellschaft. These concepts are hard to translate into English. 'Community' and 'Society' are among the labels attempted.

In essence Gemeinschaft describes the traditional groupings to which people knew they belonged: family; village; tribe. No choice was involved. What is more, people were connected to each other as whole persons, warts and all.

Tönnies recognised the psychological complement to this social reality. His term at the personal level

A caza de dientes.

III. *The alienation of feelings from actions*

was Wesenwille ('natural will'), exemplified in direct, spontaneous and integrated behaviour.

In contrast Gesellschaft has increasingly become the basis of modern society, a trend long developing but reaching its climax in what we have defined as modernity.

In Gesellschaft all relations become contractual. What is more each contract only involves the one aspect of the persons involved that is relevant – say as shareholders or as employers/employees. They are not required to be relations between whole people.

At the personal, psychological, level Tönnies uses the term Kürwille. Its root implies choice. For rational choosing is the core of this 'modern' attitude. One chooses to enter contracts; chooses which association to join; even chooses ones friends, often on the basis of perceived advantage.

Quite apart from what this does to us, we are then at the mercy of other people's choices. The effects on us are wide ranging: the choice of a prospective employer not to hire us; the nightmare traffic jam because umpteen others have chosen that journey; the feeling that a friend is not being sincere.

The word for this new social condition is alienation – hence the title of Pappenheim's book.

Many thinkers have written on alienation. A central pivot of Marx's critique of capitalism was the alienation of workers from the fruits of their labour, confronting them as commodities.

The debate among sociologists and others is whether this social and psychological transformation can be reversed – which feeds into our broader concerns.

The Game

In *The Limitations of Enlightenment Science*[22] attention was drawn to the arguments of Paul Shepard – notably in his last book *Coming Home to The Pleistocene*[23] – that our hunter-scavenger-gatherer ancestors lived in balance with nature in their scattered human groups during the Pleistocene era. (In the earlier part of this period they were mainly scavenger-gatherers since they were no match for the great hunters.)

One concept in Paul Shepard's narrative seems very puzzling at first sight: when he talks about 'the game'. Surely survival was a matter of life and death?

To grasp this notion consider a football match in which the other team was corralled into a particular area on the pitch (as was really the case in the age of animal husbandry and agriculture). Then 'our team' can score as many goals as we like – except that it wouldn't really be a game anymore. Our control would be total. Back on the savanna the contest was always in doubt.

A Modest Humanity

Attempting to draw all these strands together, we can again ask the question: what factors could lend hope for the future of our threatened Planet, even at this eleventh hour?

I believe that the core need is a more modest humanity: modest in *numbers*; modest in *behaviours*; modest in *attitudes*.

Taking the third aspect first, we are talking values: a values shift in favour of all life. With this possibility in mind we have noted some hopeful elements.

➢ A growing disenchantment among some with the dominant ideology of modernism with its tarnished promise and (at least in part of our divided selves) a yearning to be in touch with immanent values.

➢ Better understanding of social structure and our interconnectedness in it, to combat isolating individualism: an educational project here.

➢ The prospect of widespread values flips when appropriate triggers are in place, such that minority values and attitudes may become mainstream almost overnight.

➢ Recognising that the complementary nature of Divergent (leaderful) and Convergent (followful) social types not only challenges elitism but also individualism: another educational project.

➢ Growing awareness of the distress of our Planet is slowly penetrating our psyches. However this is presently focused on the threat to humans, with the average temperature rise due to greenhouse gas emissions taken as the critical measure.

Challenging Each Other

Part of the needed response is to actually change our behaviours: values are one thing but behaviours are another. We all know the expression "they voted with their wallets". Alienation is not only our remoteness from each other but our separation from ourselves.

Here part of the answer may lie in social interaction. One aspect of individualist freedom is that we don't challenge each other enough.

I like to think of myself as rooting for the planet and living (by First World standards) fairly modestly. Yet i know how resistant i felt to giving up milk (for example) despite believing that methane from cattle is potentially a far bigger threat than carbon dioxide (CO_2). In contrast i am horrified that people are still flying. Yet, apart from holiday indulgences, i know that many values focused allies would be distraught at not being able to visit relatives and friends on the other side of the World.

So i think i am arguing for a new climate of fear-less challenging of each other, coupled with 'behaviour pacts': "I will quit flying by such and such date if you will renounce animal fats/imported clothes/non-recyclables/whatever by the same target date." Giving ourselves a time window is a bit of a cop-out that doesn't do our biosphere any favours. Yet it may be more realistic in terms of human psychology and our need to adjust our heads.

Of course there will be those, especially of a 'blame the baddies' mentality, who argue for a structural approach: that such personal sacrifices are pointless while corporations and governments push mass consumption and destructive technologies, including armaments, as part of their modernist agenda.

The Numbers Question

So we come to the third great challenge: modesty in numbers.

If we accept that there are limits to what smarter technologies can achieve for a human population of 7-10 billion people.

If we accept that, even with a will, there are limits to what modest – or rather spartan – consumption can achieve for our Planet with these numbers.

Then, from a Planet Centred viewpoint the human numbers question can no longer be avoided, however emotive the issue.

First, a few facts to set the scene.[24]

➢ Estimated total human population around 10,000 BCE (at the dawn of sustained agriculture): approx. one million.

➢ Estimated populations today of some of the great apes, our close cousins, and ourselves:

  o Orang-utans: 45,000 – 69,000; falling

  o Gorillas: 156,00 – 200,000; falling

  o Chimpanzees: 172,7000 – 299,700; falling

  o Bonobos: 29,500 – 50,000; falling

  o Homo sapiens: 7,700,000,000; rising

The Sixth Extinction

More significant even than climate change is the extinction rate across all species. This is now estimated to be running at around one thousand times[25] the background rate for the last million years or so, almost entirely due to human numbers and activity.

Living Longer

Now even among the minority willing to accept human numbers as the most critical factor in pressure on the biosphere the focus has been on the *birth rate*, already contributing to falling population in some parts of the World.

Optimists believe that the combined effect of rising human living standards, more widespread contraception and the empowerment of women will cause human population to peak soon after 2050 CE, in line with the original Club of Rome[26] predictions. (Other estimates suggest human population still rising to 2100 CE when it may pass 12 billion.) Further, rising living standards implies higher consumption per head which in turn assumes that the resources will be there and certainly puts more pressure on remaining natural habitats.

Whichever population curve is accepted as the best estimate and whichever argument is considered the stronger, it is the birth rate that is seen as the key variable. The unmentionable factor in population pressure is the falling *death rate* – billions living longer than ever before.

There are two ends to this burning candle. At the front end the dramatic falls in infant and child mortality (in Victorian England for example) meant that most of the (commonly) ten children were now to survive, leading (after a time-lag of a generation or so) to decisions to have smaller families. Also, in industrialised countries there was the wealth to import the food needed to cope with the population surge.

The impact of better sanitation and medical facilities is now being felt – patchily – across the World, including in parts of Africa, leading some to believe that the same sequence of events will follow. There are good reasons for doubting this. First, we can note powerful cultural and political factors working against smaller families, from patriarchal social relations to governments viewing larger populations as potentially greater economic and military power. Secondly, there is no longer a diaspora of less developed nations to provide the cheap food needed to respond to the population surge. These *are* the less developed nations.

Despite claims of agricultural miracles and green revolutions (ultimately based on oil) the signs of limits are there. India has become a net exporter of food but with total dependence on fertilisers and also on pesticides due to the drastic reduction in varieties cultivated[27]. The reference given acknowledges some of these issues yet does not address the longer term including topsoil loss and pollution issues.

Norman Borlaug, the 'Father of The Green Revolution' is on record as saying that this 'miracle' only buys humanity a little time.

The growing bush meat trade in Africa is a reflection of desperation in the face of rising food prices. Bush meat hunting, along with habitat destruction for cash crops (including timber) is a very direct threat to particular species and to ecosystems. One might add that the political conflicts now raging across much of the World are not just about egos and ideologies: they are also resource wars as seven billion plus humans compete for a share of the cake.

Values in Tension

This narrative, starting with the improved survival rates of infants and young children, sheds a glaring light on the contrast between human centred and Planet Centred moralities.

From a human standpoint what could be a greater cause for joy than a mother *not* seeing her child dying of malaria or diarrhoea or malnutrition or other condition?

What could be more fulfilling for the aid worker than to play a part in this?

From a Planet Earth standpoint what could be more frightening than yet another pressure point on an already stressed ecosystem with so many threatened species and species webs?

Death Phobia

At the other end of the thread of life the ego desire to defeat – or at least postpone – death links up with medical advances and First World wealth. For some, life expectation is now way beyond the notional 'three score years and ten'.

Despite the enormous social cost of keeping some of us alive 'at all costs'; despite our collective exposure to end of life illnesses and conditions that were formerly hardly known; despite the 'house blocking' that contributes to the young being often unable to commence family life; despite total population pressure on ecosystems being increased by eighty million persons per year … our egos are totally supported by cultural norms that emphasise the value and preciousness of individual human life. (Except in war of course. Then state decreed enemies can be targeted; citizens killed fighting those enemies become posthumous heroes.)

IV. *Lobbying Westminster*

Actual World Population Numbers
(source: World Population Clock)

World Equivalent Population Numbers
Taking account of consumption

First World Population: 1 Billion People

Fraction of these beyond Seventy Years
2 Billion People Equivalent

First World Population
12 Billion People Equivalent
(source: Physics fact book/money)

Rest of World Population
6.7 Billion People

Rest of World Population
6.7 Billion People Equivalent

V. *Population, Consumption and Longevity – Visual Representations (not to scale)*

44

Not only do these cultural norms approve of preserving and extending life in these ways, they direct vitriolic hostility upon any who challenge this consensus, for whatever reason. Assisting someone who wants to die, even for quality of life reasons, is still a crime in many legal systems. So dying for the planet is simply off the scale.

Changing the Culture

I now argue for a cultural shift from '(try to) live forever' mode to 'self-restraint' mode: that we take the needs of our planet and its life web into account when taking responsibility for our own death, deciding when we should go. Those of us who feel ready and able to do this can feel that we are playing our part in mitigating the pressures of *high consumption longevity.*

Two important qualifiers here. First, that this step should be voluntary – definitely no eugenics – and not state imposed, though taking the views of those close to us into account. This would become more achievable as hopefully an ecocentric attitude towards individual death develops in local populations.

Second, it is within the so-called developed world that economies based on plundered wealth have enabled both high consumption and artificially extended lifespans to become realities. This approach would not be applicable in most of the 'developing world' where poverty and related factors already keep life expectancies low.

There are existing calls for a culture of restraint in bringing new human life into the world. Thus a culture of restraint at both ends of life is morally consistent – after a full life make space: don't take more than your share.

Words Matter

All values struggles, all struggles for the acceptance of new social attitudes, are fought out first in the realm of language.

In the long struggle for female emancipation words with put down intent such as 'bluestocking', 'slag', 'broad', 'flighty', 'featherbrained' and so on had to be either overcome or neutralised. Again in the realm of race 'nigger', intended as an epithet, is now used ironically between black comrades. In sexual politics, other-defined 'queer' was challenged by self-defined 'gay'. And so on.

So words matter. In the arena of self-chosen death we values warriors need to make a distinction between those who want out for reason of terminal illness, great suffering, abysmal quality of life or deep depression: in Nietzschean terms saying 'no' to life …and those of us who still value life (say 'yes' to life) yet know that they can consider their life project sufficiently complete that on balance they want to make space on this Planet for others, whether their children's children or other life forms or Gaia. In both cases the counsel of close friends who understand them well is to be valued above cultural correctness and state imposed laws.

Since words matter the commonly understood label of suicide – stripped of pejorative value judgements – can remain appropriate for those wanting out because they can no longer say 'yes' to life. When you *don't* want to go but you know that you should, a new word, a new description, will need to be brought into circulation and argued for.

An early candidate might be 'sacrifice' but i think that this smacks of ego-centred heroics. As my contribution to the debate i have suggested elsewhere 'project completion' or simply 'job done'.

I have to leave it to other values warriors to consider, arrive at and argue for a simple but potent word (or words) for what is clearly *not* suicide.

Towards a Planet Centred Culture

The earlier exploration of social structure and social flow in this essay, more extensively in *VFOT*, attempted to show that 'Human nature' is not fixed. The values of cultures, of societies, can and do evolve, for better or worse. If the triggers that usher in different values and behaviour in social situations and ecological contexts could be understood – not just intellectually but in out bones – then dramatically different situation responses would become possible.

What may now be viewed as eccentric behaviour may become – especially when Divergent led – not just socially acceptable but a new cultural norm within an increasingly Planet Centred culture. To repeat a hypothetical quote from the essay *VFOT*: "Did people once want to live forever Mummy?"

Wider Questions

This narrative has led us to a place where one answer to our question "Which Values?" could be "the values of the whole; the purpose of the whole towards self-experiencing its greatest possible complexity, diversity and beauty".

This explanation certainly makes sense of the whole thrust of physical and organic evolution, at least as observed in this particular corner of the Universe: ever greater complexity and endless cascades of new emergent properties.

By making this suggestion we have strayed into the realm of Cosmology – the big questions.

One of the many limitations of Enlightenment science[28] is its claim to be values free: "others have ideologies; we deal in facts". As has been pointed out any statement of 'fact' is based on its (often invisible) starting assumptions about the world in which events are happening and situations occur. Further, Enlightenment science has always been wary of, dismissive of, cosmology – questions beyond measurement and control. Yet these include life's big questions.

By way of an example consider (as Nietzsche did) the amazing way that music can sometimes move us. To say that the 'evolution' of music was/is an emergent property is a truism that does not get us very far. Following Terrence Deacon's[29] claim that Homo sapiens has become the Symbolic Species, could it be that music is capable of taking us below our symbols games to a truer Self (in the Jungian sense)? Or could it be that through the poignant identification with suffering and joy by creatures such as ourselves, our Universe is able to see a reflection of itself? Was this even the point all along?

Some Answers?

When it comes to contemplating 'our' Universe as a dynamic whole there are arguably three explanations offered.

The first is that the Universe is simply a beautiful machine behaving according to its 'laws' (read patterns) and needs no further explanation. As explored in *Limitations*[30] this interpretation encounters problems in the fields of quantum uncertainty, the evolution of life and subjectivity. However, these are not the point here: it is a complete cosmology – a big picture assumption.

The second, and very ancient, explanation is that The Universe is sustained and guided by an 'external' wisdom with a purpose (read morality) of its own. In most descriptions this guiding force is named as God.

The third understanding, which stems from Schopenhauer's insight and is argued for in these essays, is that the driving purpose (morality) is internal: our Universe wills and suffers, just as its parts do, as we do.

It is unlikely that there is an absolute sense in which any such cosmology could be proved correct. The validity of any of them will be relative to our own standpoint.

Values and Evolution

Now we know from the record of biological evolution on this Planet that there were and are plenty of dead ends. It is a moot point whether some of these could be seen as wrong turnings rather than simply 'running out of niche'.

Humans? It was made clear in *VFOT* that Homo sapiens (us), with our aggrandising morality, have already crossed the second threshold defined by Ivan Illich; are

VI. *The Ancient of Days – William Blake*

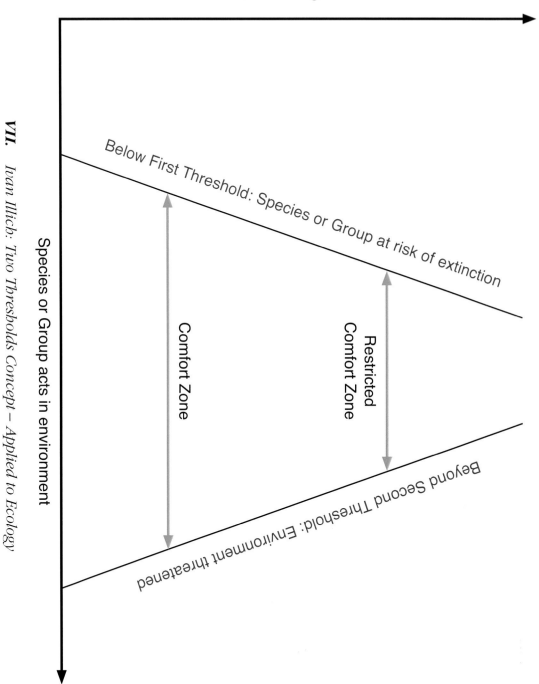

VII. *Ivan Illich: Two Thresholds Concept – Applied to Ecology*

Poorer, more fragile environment

Species or Group acts in environment

Below First Threshold: Species or Group at risk of extinction

Comfort Zone

Restricted Comfort Zone

Beyond Second Threshold: Environment threatened

now a threat to all life on this Planet. The question must be asked as to whether this is due to the values we hold, have held, or whether we are an evolutionary wrong turning that offends the purpose of our Universe.

The Victorian age in the West, and especially in England, was the great age of optimism. Despite social flaws confidence abounded in all things. It was said that: "God is an Englishman and in His Heaven".

This optimism extended to evolutionary theory: onwards and upwards with humans at the pinnacle of that great story. The philosopher Herbert Spencer[31] incorporated the principles of Darwinian biological evolution into a broader theory that included social evolution. This was highly influential at the time and still has adherents today. For example the notion that we (humans) are evolving towards a group mind and need to become conscious of that purpose[32].

It was noted in *VFOT* that this era ended in the period around the First World War with the birth of pessimism – notably among sensitives and artists – and the advent of Postmodernism. It went wider than that. My Father taught me the mantra of the squaddies in the trenches: "Praise the Lord ... and pass the ammunition".

The positive side of this sea change – for some – is a new spirit of humility and uncertainty that could in due course bode well for the growth of less homocentric values.

It is of course too soon to say that Modernism, still arrogant and optimistic despite the evidence, is dead in the water.

The Broad Context

So we see that the struggle of values warriors to advance Planet Centred values can be placed in a much wider context. The possibility, at least, that our Universe knows all, suffers all, is enchanted by all, is purposed to enhance all.

We may or may not be able to harness this understanding in our efforts to encourage values that are centred on our biosphere. Yet maybe we *can* feel that we are "on the side of the angels".

A POST-OPTIMISM REVIEW

The optimistic undertone of the above writing needs to be doubted in the light of increased awareness of the total situation on Planet Earth and of the reality of highly integrated systems with their own logic and momentum.

Bionic Escape?

Before facing up to this possible future one aspect of the "technology will save us" attitude not fully explored before should now be examined.

Given that some zones of Planet Earth may become uninhabitable for biological humans in a possible future; given the apparently limitless reach of scientific/technological progress ... the idea of 'human' transition into a post-organic future is being put forward by some.

What could this mean? Who or what would these transition beings be? Who is seeking this symbolic victory?

The last question is perhaps the easiest to answer. It would be the quest of our symbolic selves, our ego-identities, determined to survive at all costs – one could say programmed to do so. The elimination of the physical suffering self would simply be collateral damage in the project.

There are two realms in which the attempted transition could be carried forward.

The first of these would be physical robots (for want of a better word). Such bionic beings would need to be constructed, programmed, sustained, repaired.

It is not hard to spot the difficulties. Apart from physical and logistical problems, the ego-I would need to be either transplanted into the new more robust shell or duplicated/cloned in order to maintain 'our' continuity.

Lack of a reproductive system would be a lesser problem since the ego-I wants to live for ever.

From our humble organic human perspective this would be a dystopian vision – though hardly more so than cold war planning for mutually assured nuclear destruction (M.A.D.) in order to avoid ego defeat on life's chess board. (We all came very close to this outcome in 1962.)

The second route to 'eternal life' would supposedly be 'our' transference into a virtual reality, into the ether. In this case it becomes even harder to visualise our symbolic selves maintaining continuity of identity, let alone keeping our ego pride intact.

Beyond Optimism

In *The Limitations of Enlightenment Science*[33] the foundations of that science were questioned on several levels.

Perhaps not sufficiently emphasised has been the brittle optimism underpinning its perspectives. No one saw this more clearly than Friedrich Nietzsche. As early as 1872 he foresaw the limiting contradictions that are now apparent to some perceptive observers. The following short excerpt from *The Birth of Tragedy*[34] is worth presenting:

"But now, spurred on by its powerful illusion, science is rushing irresistibly to its limits, where the optimism essential to logic collapses. For the periphery of the circle of science has an infinite number of points, and while it is as yet impossible to tell how the circle could ever be fully measured, the noble, gifted man, even before the mid-course of his life, inevitably reaches that peripheral boundary, where he finds himself staring into the ineffable. If he sees there, to his dismay, how logic twists around itself and finally bites itself in the tail, there dawns a new form of knowledge, tragic knowledge ..."

Nietzsche might have had David Bohm in mind: an eminent theoretical physicist whose recognition of the ineffable took him beyond scientific orthodoxy – to the dismay of former colleagues – and to explore notions of an underlying 'implicate order' with sages such as Jiddu Krishnamurti and 'beyond the pale' academics. His dialogue with Rupert Sheldrake was referred to in *Limitations*.[35]

Superorganisms

The academic work of John Gowdy and Lisi Krall[36] suggests that species having highly integrated mass societies may have a momentum of their own way beyond the influence of individual members. Hence the notion of the superorganism.

It is not hard to see that an increasingly integrated human culture of nearly eight billion people could be classed as a superorganism: a whole entity in which the previous argument for our existence on the interface between autonomy and collectivity breaks down. Feedback loops through which human agency may act to modify the direction of travel can become less effective or even illusory.

Add to this the increasing evidence of the intense pressure of human population density: resource conflicts, social breakdowns, biosphere degradation … and re-assessments of priorities by values warriors are called for.

Certainly the efforts of many concerned humans to attempt to avert the alleged tipping points remain valid: both because the above assumptions may be wrong after all and because they represent intrinsic human behaviour regardless of instrumental outcomes. More on this last point below.

Having said this, it is argued now that at least some of us need to visualise a transformational scenario. Given that no one can predict the future for certain what trajectory can we guess at?

Three Phases

I am suggesting now three possible stages or sequences for the future of this biosphere and its human and non-human passengers:

➢   A Stress Period

➢   A Chaos Period

VIII.   *Tsunami Wave Crashing*

➢   A Remnants Period

Expanding on these: -

A. Stress

This stage is already upon us. The signs are everywhere. Not here just thinking about the gathering storm clouds of natural events. Rather the early indications of social and psychological breakdown. More brittle, less tolerant social attitudes; less trust in 'democratic' structures; the social consequences of mass migrations; a resurgence of human trafficking and the slave trade; the me-me of identity politics; the escalation of mental health issues ... the list goes on.

B. Chaos

A terrible time approaching in which millions, possibly billions, of humans will die prematurely. (Other species and life forms are already vanishing.) Breakdown of world economic, logistical and knowledge infrastructure. Frantic final struggles for resources. War lord hegemonies competing with the elite cores of former states for local dominance. 'Last man standing' conflicts.

Amidst this chaos isolated pockets of human groups seeking to survive through co-operation plus both self-imposed and situation imposed austerity.

C. Remnants

Some biological survivors, including some humans, trying to cope with and adapt to a partially wrecked planet on which temperature and other parameters are well outside previous comfort zones. The values which any surviving humans embody, will determine their relationship with other surviving biology as all still living species attempt to find niches and recover from the extinction.

Which Values?

Arguing now that there are two fundamental sets of values or attitudes that are critical as we face the future. The second group, following on from the thread above, may be summed up in the simple imperative: "Learn to lose!" This will be addressed below. Meanwhile the first value set is applicable to both the implicitly optimistic "we can act to turn it round" scenario as well as the "prepare to adapt for a different world" assumptions.

Intrinsic Behaviour v Instrumental Behaviour

Earlier in the story i suggested that as part of a culture of restraint some individuals might choose a non-suicidal exit from the planet after a full life, to make space for others, for the unborn, for the future of all life. To do this even before any cultural shift in values endorsed such actions.

The response of some readers to this suggestion could well be that a few people contemplating such actions would be utterly futile amidst a world population approaching eight billions.

This last response goes to the heart of instrumental behaviour: that all actions, including moral actions, should be judged by their likely consequences, and chosen (or not) accordingly.

As was observed earlier in the section on Ferdinand Tönnies such a response would be part of the way of being in the world that he labelled as Kürwille: chosen, calculated behaviour. In contrast, when your actions are intrinsic, you feel them to be right; no calculation of benefit is made or needed. This was Tönnies understanding of Wesenwille. It was noted that the multiplied consequence of calculating behaviour was Gesellschaft, the contract society, the alienated society.

The inference in terms of social action is that striving for the better world you believe in, doing it in the way that feels right, will always be intrinsically valid even if your efforts should be in vain.

The Superorganism Revisited

Following on from the earlier reference citing the work of John Gowdy and Lisi Krall[37]. The implication taken here is that an integrated economy of nearly eight billion humans may be considered as a superorganism in the sense they defined.

However in their work the example species offered was the leaf cutter ant – far removed from the species Homo sapiens.

The core argument was that within a mass organisation the whole has a momentum and trajectory of its own, not amenable to individual or small group decisions. So how valid is the comparison with a mass humanity?

It has been a core proposition of the social theory offered in these essays that humans, in a traditional group context, sit astride the interface between individuality and collectivity.

An obvious difference between ourselves and ants (we presume) is that humans are capable of overview – of forming a mental picture of the total situation, with the prospect of acting to change that situation.

However there are several challenges. The first rests on the distinction between *individuality* – a capacity for autonomous thought and action – and *individualism* – a motivation based on individual self-interest.

Attention has been drawn elsewhere to a benign effect of individual self-interest cited by Adam Smith[38] with his 'invisible hand': that the total effect of individuals pursuing self interest in the market place can be economic benefit

IX.   Leaf Cutter Ants

for all through their exchanges. The counter example given was a fire in a night club (say) where individual efforts by people to save themselves by rushing the doors can lead to catastrophic loss of life,

In both cases the collective result does not reflect the intentions of the individuals involved.

Where individuals do seem to be willing to co-operate in order to effect change their motivations may be complex. For each person or sub group there may be a social or economic price – especially if it involves hardship – that some will not feel willing to pay.

Beyond this there is the question of *agency*: having the leverage to effect a desired change. This becomes the critical issue in a 'superorganism' approaching eight billion interconnected yet disparate human individuals.

Lacking true agency we can note the various strategies that the most concerned people and groups may resort to.

The first of these is simply setting out the facts: the consequences of failing to address a particular problem (say rising carbon dioxide levels or species habitat destruction). The "warning to humanity" by 20,000 scientists[39] is a classic example.

Related to this is the strategy of exhortation: "unless we act now ..." Those who make such exhortations are often bemused by the lack of response. Their understanding of human psychology is minimal.

A third strategy is to look to enforcement action by governments or supra-governmental groupings. Again this shows lack of understanding of what 'The State' is and the various lobby pressures acting on governance. Some understand better than others the power of vested interests, including multi-nationals beyond the control of individual jurisdictions. Less recognised is the democratic 'lobby' of electorates taught to have (proxy) power without responsibility and expecting to be bribed with goodies for their votes.

Yet another strategy (if that is the word) is looking for technology as a saviour. Technology may in fact be able to provide short term relief – to buy a little time – in some instances. Increasing stratospheric reflectivity could be an example. However, this is straying beyond the topic.

So the central feature of a superorganism is the lack of agency to effect a change of direction. *If this is our case then the full consequences of a planetary transition will need to be faced.*

Learning to Lose?

In several of the essays in this series attention has been drawn to the two thresholds concept of Ivan Illich as it applies to species in biological evolution – that below a lower threshold a species fails to survive in its environment, whilst above an upper threshold its success becomes a threat to that environment.

Modern humans and our forebears, as an evolving species, have spent several billion years learning to win – to stay above the survival threshold. Our new hard lesson is learning to lose – to not exceed the second (environmental destruction) threshold.

This is where the wisdom of Paul Shepard – and many traditional peoples – becomes relevant: foregoing the attempt to control; accepting the game of life on a level playing field.

Psychologically speaking this is a scary challenge. Control is not just, or even mainly, about military dominance – nor even technological dominance in the field.

The underlying aim of Enlightenment science (for instance) is to understand, to measure, to assess in order to increase our control of situations. Hence the somewhat tongue in cheek rebuke to all scientists in *VFOT*: "Stop measuring – at least on Thursdays!"

In *The Limitations of Enlightenment Science* it was pointed out that the Romantic Movement poets and artists saw clearly the direction in which the arrogance of Enlightenment science was heading. A reference to

Goethe's Faust was made[40] in which Faust makes his pact with the Devil 'for the right to control nature'.

It could be mentioned that the concluding section of *Limitations* outlines a similar post transformation reality, with a more optimistic undertone yet still emphasising the values of modesty, humility and empathy.

Going forward, the mantra for any surviving humans could be: "*Less knowledge, more wisdom*". This along with the imperative: "***Learn to lose***". A more nuanced rendering of this command would be "*Forego Total Control*".

*   *   *   *   *   *   *   *   *

As for my own position i have little to add to the personal end note of *VFOT*, except that i failed to make the eightieth year deadline. Extracting from this: -

"… as a values warrior i am beginning to pass the baton. Although i am not deaf to the arguments of friends and comrades, my provisional decision is to exit the planet, to melt back into the Universe, at the age of eighty …"

This was written when i had little understanding of the practical difficulties involved amidst a hostile culture.

Woody Wood   December 2019

REFERENCE NOTES

1. *Values for Our Time*   B.A. Wood *Devolve!*   2014 paperback ISBN 978 0993112607

2. *VFOT* page 7; makes reference to *Cargo Cult Science* Richard Feynman in Engineering and Science N 37, June 1974, pp 10-13

3. *The World as Will and Idea* Arthur Schopenhauer Everyman 1995 paperback ISBN 0460875051

4. *Biology as Ideology* Richard Lewontin Harper Collins 1993 paperback ISBN 978 0060975197

5. *The Ego and The Id*   Sigmund Freud   Dover Publications 2018 paperback ISBN 978 0486821566 Freud presents the Ego as a mediator between the drives of the Id, the (internalised) social pressure to conform and external reality. But "every means strives to become an end". The Ego as the Symbolic Self (ref Terrence Deacon) can develop its own power agenda.

6. *The Medium, The Mystic and The Physicist* Lawrence Leshan   Turnstone Books   1974 paperback   SBN 855000384

7. *Life Against Death: The Psychoanalytic Meaning of History*   Norman O. Brown Wesleyan U.P. 1986 paperback ISBN 0819561444

8. *On the Genealogy of Morality* F. Nietzsche Cambridge U.P. 1994 paperback pp 165-168 and other references. ISBN 978 0521406102

9. extract from 1971 essay, B.A. Wood in *International Associations* UAI 1975 Nr 2 (February)

10. *Mind the Gap* Ferdinand Mount Short Books 2012 edition paperback ISBN 978 1906021955

11. *Instincts of The Herd in Peace and War* Wilfred Trotter Pranava Books 2009 paperback ISBN 978 1150070048

12. Executive and Sensory method still applied at Braziers School of Integrative Social Research www.braziers. org

13. *VFOT* Pages 28 ff

14. *VFOT* Page 41 and Plate 6; also note 46

15. *Social Psychology and Individual Values* D.W. Harding Brill Publishers 1966 paperback ISBN 978 0090426324

16. Ditto pages 15 ff

17. *Ecological Ethics: An Introduction* Patrick Curry Polity Press 2011 paperback ISBN 978 0745651262 Second updated edition 2018

18. *Deep Roots in A Time of Frost - Essays on Tolkien* Patrick Curry Walking Tree Books 2014 paperback ISBN 978 3905703337

19. *Enchantment – Wonder in Modern Life* Patrick Curry Floris Books 2019 paperback ISBN 978 1782506096

20. *The Alienation of Modern Man* Fritz Pappenheim Monthly Review Press 1968 paperback SBN 853450056

21. *Community and Society* Ferdinand Tönnies Dover Publications 2002 paperback ISBN 978 0486424972

22. *The Limitations of Enlightenment Science* B.A. Wood *Devolve!* 2017 paperback   ISBN 978 0993112638

23. *Coming Home to The Pleistocene* Paul Shepard Island Press 1998 paperback ISBN 978 1559635905

24. Human Population Estimate 10,000 BCE: Vaughn's Summaries: World Population Growth History Chart; Present Great Ape Populations: World Atlas, 2017 update.

25. Wikipedia: Extinction Page

26. *The Limits to Growth* Report to The Club of Rome from the Massachusetts Institute of Technology Pan Books 1975 paperback ISBN 0330241699 The original predictions, although often updated, have proved durable.

27. www.thoughtco.com/green-revolution-overview-1434948

28. An example is referred to in note 4 above.

29. *The Symbolic Species: Co-evolution of Language and The Brain* T.W. Deacon W.W. Norton & Co 1997 paperback ISBN 978 0393317541

30. *The Limitations of Enlightenment Science* See note 22 above. Some difficulties discussed: Subjectivity, pages 58-59; Quantum theory, pages 68-70; Evolution of life, pages 72-73.

31. *The Principles of Sociology: Volumes 1, 2 & 3* Herbert Spencer Routledge 2001 paperback ISBN 978 0765807502

32. Braziers School of Integrative Social Research www. braziers.org

33. *The Limitations of Enlightenment Science* See note 22 above.

34. *The Birth of Tragedy* Friedrich Nietzsche Penguin Classics 1993 paperback ISBN 978 0140433395

35. *A New Science of Life* (3rd edition) Rupert Sheldrake Icon Books 2009 paperback ISBN 978 1848310241 Appendix B: *Morphic Fields and The Implicate Order* A dialogue with David Bohm.

36. *The Ultrasocial Origin of The Anthropocene* John M. Gowdy and Lisi Krall in Ecological Economics 95 pp137-147 November 2013 also refer to The Economic Legacy of The Holocene Lisi Krall in *The Ecological Citizen* volume 2, issue 1 pages 67-76 ISSN 2515-1967

37. Ibid

38. *The Wealth of Nations* Adam Smith (modern translation) Industrial Systems Research 2015 paperback ISBN 978 0906321706

39. World Scientists' Warning to Humanity: Second Warning 2017 in AIBS *Bioscience* Volume 67, Issue 12, Dec 2017 pages 1026-1028

40. *Philosophy for Beginners* Richard Osborne and Ralph Edney Writers and Readers Publishing Inc. 1992 paperback ISBN 978 0863161575 Page 99